Pube Topiary

The Ultimate Guide to Manscaping and Bush Trimming

Lotta Bush

INTRODUCTION

Say goodbye to boring pubes with this book of 11 top ideas to help you style those hairs into something a little more impressive.

Designs increase in difficulty as you move through the book so start at the beginning and work your way through to peak pube-fection.

We recommend drawing the designs first in something washable and kind to skin such as body pens or eyeliner. For some of the trickier designs you may wish to trace the designs onto paper and cut out templates to 'work' around.

Then, simply use your pube-approved hair removal method of choice and wonder at your new found artistic skill. Remember to stay safe and never use anything that isn't approved for genital use in your nether regions!

STRIPES

This simple design is perfect for the beginner stylist. Classic, angular and 100% chic.

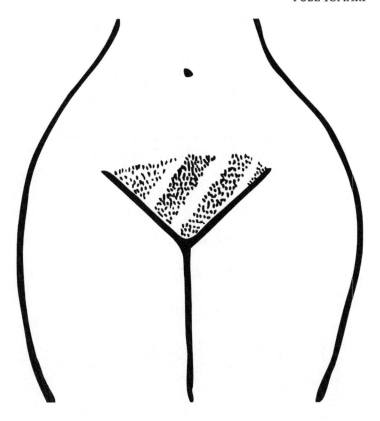

X MARKS THE SPOT

Arr me hearties! Guide the world to your treasure with this basic design.

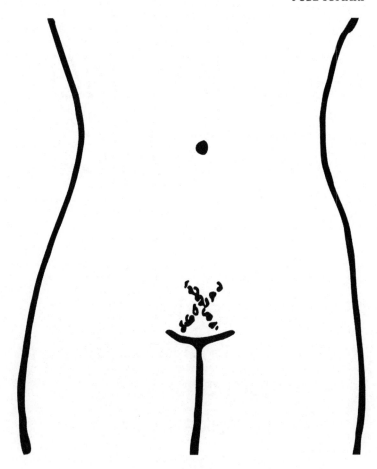

CLOWNING AROUND

This beginner design calls for an untamed bush as the hair of our circus character. A simple circle below makes the shiny red nose.

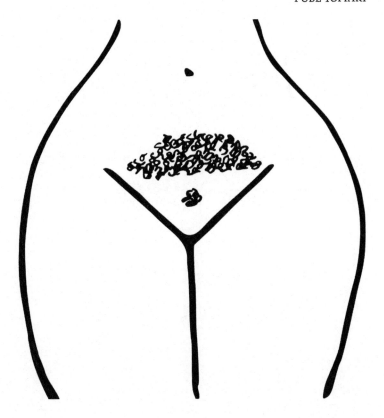

THE BOWIE

Channel your inner superstar with this bolt from the blue. Also, a good choice for fans of a certain boy wizard.

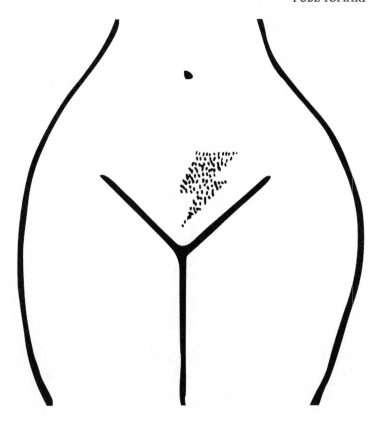

HIS AND HERS

Nothing says 'I love you' quite like matching half-heart shaped pubes. Show your partner that your heart is only whole when they are around.

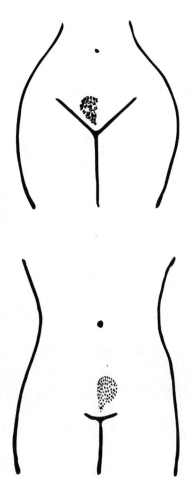

ASK ME A QUESTION

This design is perfect for the inquisitive 'scaper. Is it a whimsical pubic pattern or is it a commentary on the uncertainty of life as we know it? Who knows...

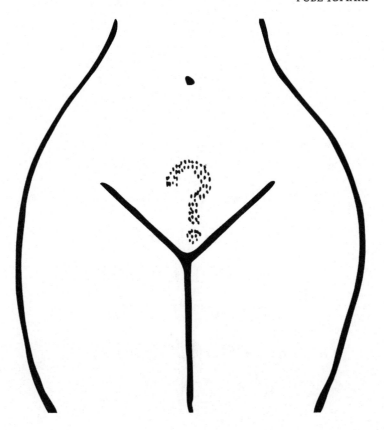

PUSSY CAT

Celebrate man's favourite feline friend with this cute kitty design. Perfect for cat lovers and those who just like a good pussy pun.

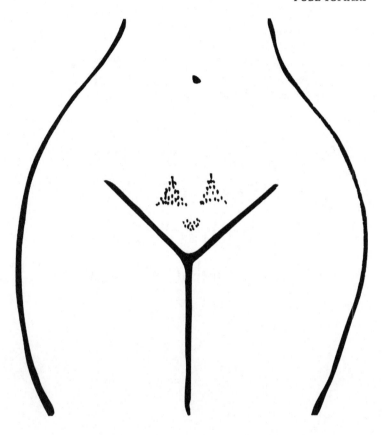

HOT SPOT

Show the world that you've got a full signal with this 21st century pubic design.

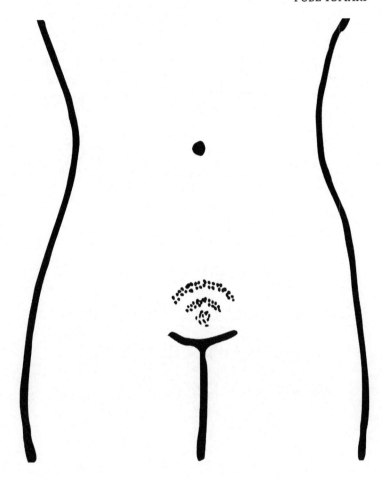

PUBE-TINTED GLASSES

You've heard of eyes in the back of your head. Now you can have eyes in the front of your... well...you know...

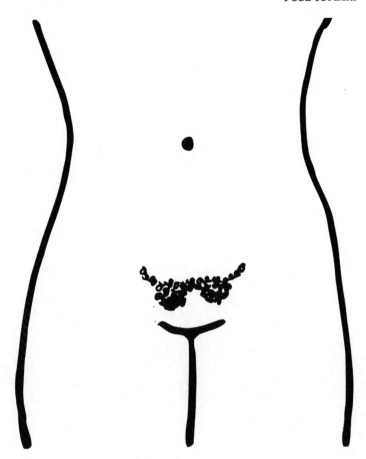

PRIZE WINNER

Do you want to feel like a winner every time you jump in the shower? Style yourself your own winner's rosette for that 'top of the podium' feeling.

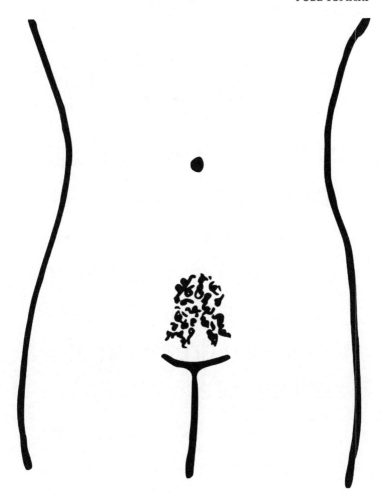

THE EDEN

This expert design will take you right back to biblical times as you channel your inner Adam or Eve. Perfect for those dreaming of a simpler life.

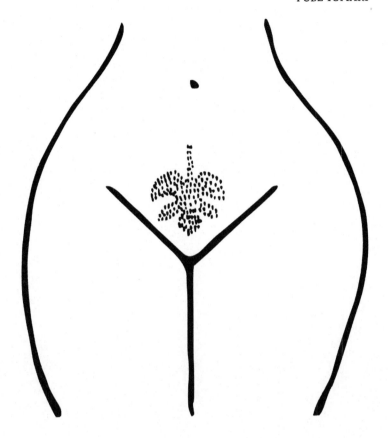

EPILOGUE

Thank you for reading, I hope this book has started you on a journey of pube-discovery. Do feel free to explore further and come up with your own designs.

Lotta Bush

Printed in Great Britain
by Amazon